Praise for the Book

"Gordon Murray and Dan Goldie have written a book that every American should read. Its clarity de-mystifies the investment process and its insights can make anyone who reads it a better investor."
– Bill Bradley, former United States Senator

"An excellent primer for the investor who is not a finance specialist."
– Eugene F. Fama, Robert R. McCormick Distinguished Service Professor of Finance, Chicago Booth School of Business, widely recognized as the "father of modern finance"

"Murray and Goldie use simple yet compelling logic to explain the fundamental principles of investing. Their clear advice will improve your investment experience."
– Kenneth R. French, Heidt Professor of Finance, Dartmouth College, Tuck School of Business

"I'm glad to see Gordon and Dan collect these insights into a handy, easy-to-use primer so Gordon can stop explaining these principles at Sunday brunch and family birthdays. Full disclosure: Gordon's my brother-in-law. That said, I found this slim volume incredibly helpful in explaining how to think about investing. It's reassuring to know there are some simple principles anyone can keep in mind to make decent decisions and banish the vague anxiety most of us have about where we've put our money."
– Ira Glass, Edward R. Murrow Award winner, Host of NPR's *This American Life*

"Gordon Murray and Dan Goldie share secrets that Wall Street would rather you not know. You can implement a few simple strategies at a very low cost that will outperform most of the stock picking and complicated advice hawked by high-priced brokers. Read this book and prosper."
– Joseph A. Grundfest, former SEC Commissioner, co-founder of Financial Engines, and Professor of Law and Business at Stanford Law School

"Goldie and Murray have distilled the essence of the matter, and explain in clear English, the advantages of using a fee-only financial advisor, how to select such, and how to work with one in the short and long run. This is sound advice, which you will rarely if ever get from a daily financial newscast."
– Harry M. Markowitz, PH.D., Nobel Laureate in Economics, 1990, Father of Modern Portfolio Theory

"Wow! Goldie and Murray have just hit a home run. If I could give only one book on investing to my friends and family, this one would be it."
– Bob Waterman, co-author, *In Search of Excellence*, former director of McKinsey & Company

The *Investment* Answer

LEARN TO MANAGE YOUR MONEY & PROTECT YOUR FINANCIAL FUTURE

DANIEL C. GOLDIE, CFA, CFP
& GORDON S. MURRAY

GRAND CENTRAL
PUBLISHING

NEW YORK   BOSTON

Grand Central Publishing
Hachette Book Group
1290 Avenue of the Americas
New York, NY 10104

www.HachetteBookGroup.com

Grand Central Publishing is a division of Hachette Book Group, Inc. The Grand Central Publishing name and logo are trademarks of Hachette Book Group, Inc.

The publisher is not responsible for websites (or their content) that are not owned by the publisher.

Printed in the United States of America

First Edition: January 2011

10 9 8 7 6 5 4 3

Library of Congress Control Number: 2010942432
ISBN: 9781455503308

Prologue

Wall Street brokers and active money managers use your relative lack of investment expertise to their benefit... not yours.

The financial press uses your inclination to be afraid during falling markets and confident during rising markets, to its benefit... not yours.

The record shows that our elected representatives, once-trusted ratings agencies, and government regulators have placed their own interests first... not yours.

None of these parties has demonstrated an understanding of what you are about to read in this book. It's time for you to put yourself first and take charge of your investment future. It will be much simpler than you think.

Table of Contents

Why We Wrote this Book

We hear stories like these too often:

Ron and Judy work with a broker who invested their money in some of the brokerage firm's popular investment products (a hedge fund-of-funds, a managed futures account, two separately managed stock accounts, and several municipal bonds). They have no idea what they are paying in fees, or whether their investment results have been good or bad. Their broker has not developed a long-term investment plan for them, so they don't know whether they are on track to achieve their goals. In fact, they are not even sure what their investment goals are! Their broker is now recommending a gold fund, because his firm is forecasting a rise in inflation. Ron and Judy don't know what to do.

Betty has never trusted the stock market. She and her late husband always invested their savings in bank CDs and money market funds. She now realizes that her savings have not grown enough for her to maintain her current lifestyle, and she will be largely dependent on social security income for the rest of her life. She is not sure where to turn next.

Steve manages his money through an online brokerage account, buying individual stocks. He has made a few good picks, but for the most part his portfolio has done poorly. He selects his stocks after researching companies online, watching CNBC, and reviewing financial periodicals, but feels uncertain about this approach. He is spending a lot of time on this, yet he knows that he's not really getting anywhere. He wonders whether the time he spends on his portfolio would be better spent building his career.

Amy has been contributing regularly to her company's 401(k) plan, and has also purchased some stock mutual funds with additional savings. After the stock market dropped in 2008, she sold everything in a panic and has been sitting in cash ever since. She has heard that stocks have a good long-term record, but her personal experience has not been good. She wonders if she is just not cut out to be an investor.

We want to change the way you think about investing. Clearly, the traditional financial services industry is failing to serve investors properly. Our hope is that this book will influence the way you select financial advisors, invest your money, and assess your results.

Our Story

We have a common belief about how markets work and how individuals should approach long-term investing. We came to this shared view from different places: Gordon from a successful 25-year Wall Street career interfacing with the most sophisticated institutional investors in the world, and Dan from nearly two decades of working with individual investors as an independent financial advisor. The fact that **we have come from opposite sides of the industry and have reached the same conclusions about how to invest** is a testament to the universal logic of this approach.

When we first came to appreciate the unshakable logic and compelling evidence supporting the investment concepts described in this book, each of us experienced an epiphany that we describe as a "light bulb turning on."

There are numerous other books and papers that address the ideas you are about to read here…and in far more detail. However, therein lies part of the problem. For most of us, these publications are too long or too technical. **Our goal is to express these important concepts in a way any investor can understand.** We have purposely kept this book brief and to the point. We want you to be able to get from beginning to end in one sitting!

We need a better way to invest. We need a better understanding of how Wall Street really functions and how markets work. We need to feel confident that we are investing prudently and making smart financial decisions.

There is an answer. You'll find it in this book.

Introduction

Today, the good news is that we expect to live much longer, healthier lives. The life expectancy of a newly retired, 65-year-old couple in the U.S. is more than 20 years — far longer than it was just a few decades ago. Furthermore, new medical advances are announced almost every day to enhance the quality of our lives and help us age more gracefully.

The bad news is that many of us will not have enough money to retire comfortably. In addition, we are told not to count on traditional pension plans, Social Security, or Medicare. Whether we are saving for a down payment on a house, our child's college education, or a comfortable retirement, **the need for us to invest wisely is more important now than ever**.

Some of us believe the self-serving hype from the financial media, who tell us that we can do it all ourselves. They tell us we can beat the market if we buy the mutual funds or stocks they recommend. They want us to believe that we can get rich quick if we follow their trading recommendations.

As a result, we might waste countless hours scouring the latest financial periodicals, studying brokerage house research reports, or watching the financial news, all with the hope of finding the next hot stock, superstar fund manager, or right time to jump into or out of the market. Or we may do the opposite — ignore the importance of financial planning, simply "hope for the best," or spend more time making our vacation plans than our financial plans.

Thus, most of us end up taking unnecessary risk, not diversifying our portfolios properly, and paying too much in fees and taxes — resulting in poor investment results with too *little* return and too *much* risk.

The unfortunate truth when it comes to investing is that many of us are scared and don't know where to start. Wall Street feels like a casino with the odds stacked against us. We are intimidated by the language of investments and are wary of recommendations from Wall Street research analysts. As a result, it is not hard to understand why so many of us are confused about what to do with our money and are uncertain about how to make smart financial decisions.

As a patient and disciplined investor with a longer time horizon, financial markets can become your *ally* rather than your *adversary*. **All you have to do is make five informed decisions** that will allow you to take advantage of the wisdom that Nobel Prize winners have acquired over the past six decades to stack the investment odds in your favor.

You CAN have a successful investment experience!

These decisions are:

1. The Do-It-Yourself Decision

   Should you try to invest on your own or seek help from an investment professional? And if so, which type of advisor is best?

2. The Asset Allocation Decision

   How should you allocate your investments among stocks (equities), bonds (fixed income), and cash (money market funds)?

3. The Diversification Decision

   Which specific asset classes within these broad categories should you include in your portfolio, and in what proportions?

4. The Active versus Passive Decision

   Should you favor an actively managed approach to investing that seeks to outsmart the market, or a more passive approach that delivers market-like returns?

5. The Rebalancing Decision

When should you sell certain assets in your portfolio and when should you buy more?

Each of these decisions has a significant impact on your overall investment experience. Whether you know it or not, every day you are making these decisions. Even if you decide to just stay the course and do nothing with your investment portfolio, you are inherently answering all of these five questions.

We will provide you with the necessary background to make these decisions. And to help you make smart choices, we will share our opinions and recommendations with you.

By learning how to make five informed investment decisions that capture the essence of investing, you will never again be afraid of financial markets or uncertain about what to do with your money. You will no longer be a *speculator*…you will be an *investor*.

The
Decisions

CHAPTER 1

The Do-It-Yourself Decision

DO-IT-YOURSELF

The do-it-yourself (DIY) approach is increasingly popular in some industries: home repair and renovation, decorating, self-publishing, and fashion. However — we are not going to beat around the bush here — in most cases, we do not believe it is prudent when it comes to investing. Finance is complex, the odds are stacked against you, and the stakes are very high: your entire financial future. Most people would never make serious medical decisions without consulting a doctor. We believe you should take care of your financial health the same way you take care of your physical health — with the appropriate professionals by your side!

Attempting to invest on your own can be difficult, time-consuming, and emotionally taxing. Most individual investors do not have the skills or the inclination to manage their own investments. However, even for those who do, this may not be a good idea. In today's world of global markets and complex financial instruments, professionals have access to superior resources. It is difficult for an individual investor to effectively put together and maintain an efficient portfolio that is properly diversified, minimizes fees and taxes, and avoids overlapping assets. In addition, the ongoing monitoring of your portfolio and maintenance of your desired risk exposure can be challenging and overwhelming without access to the tools that are used by competent professional financial advisors.

What's more, our own natural instincts can be our worst enemy when it comes to investing. This is illustrated in an annual study conducted by Dalbar, a leading financial services market research firm that investigates how mutual fund investors' *behavior* affects the returns they actually earn. Figure 1-1 shows data from the most recent Dalbar study covering the 20-year period ending in 2009:

- The average stock fund investor earned a paltry **3.2** percent annually versus **8.2** percent for the S&P 500 Index;

- The average bond fund investor earned only **1.0** percent annually versus the Barclays U.S. Aggregate Bond Index return of **7.0** percent; and

- What is perhaps most remarkable and unfortunate is that **the average stock fund investor barely beat inflation, and the average bond fund investor barely grew his money at all**.

Figure 1-1 Average Investor vs. Markets

January 1, 1990 to December 31, 2009

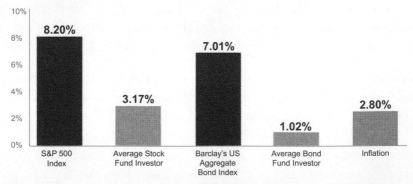

Average stock and bond investor performances were used from a DALBAR study, Quantitative Analysis of Investor Behavior (QAIB), 03/2010. QAIB calculates investor returns as the change in assets after sales, redemptions, and exchanges. This method captures realized and unrealized capital gains, dividends, interest, trading costs, sales charges, fees, expenses, and any other costs. After calculating investor returns, two percentages are calculated: total investor return for the period and annualized investor return. The fact that buy-and-hold has been a successful strategy in the past does not guarantee that it will be successful in the future.

How could this happen? The simple answer is that we tend to buy stocks and bonds after their prices have risen. We do this because we feel comfortable and confident when markets are up. Similarly, when markets have experienced a downturn, fear sets in and we are often quick to sell. This behavior can result in our **buying at or near market highs, and selling at or near market lows**, thus failing to capture even a market rate of return.

Figure 1-2 illustrates what we call the *emotional cycle of investing* and how it can cause us to make costly mistakes.

Figure 1-2 The Emotional Cycle of Investing

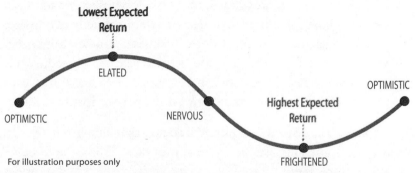

Certainly the media and the Wall Street brokerage industry are motivated to contribute to this phenomenon. As you search for your next great investment idea, you might read a financial periodical such as *Fortune*, *Forbes*, or *Money*, or you might tune into CNBC, Bloomberg, or Fox Business News, all of whom try to turn investing into entertainment. Then when the hook is in and you decide to act on some new idea, your transactions will put additional commissions in your broker's pockets. **Many financial institutions still take far too big a cut as you move your money from one hyped investment to another.**

There are many behavioral inclinations that work to our detriment as long-term investors. For example, do any of the following sound familiar?

Overconfidence. A general disposition to be overconfident can help society in many ways. For example, without this bias, many new inventions, companies, and pioneering research would never come about. However, we need to understand that overconfidence with regard to investing can be detrimental to our financial health. Success in one walk of life does not automatically translate to success in investing. Unfortunately, many highly accomplished people have learned this lesson the hard way — through severe investment losses.

Attraction to rising prices. When the prices of most consumer goods such as gasoline or beef rise, people tend to either cut back or find a substitute. However, with financial assets the opposite seems true. Many investors are more attracted to a stock whose price has risen than one whose price has fallen because we incorrectly extrapolate past price changes into the future. Likewise, mutual funds that have done the best recently are aggressively purchased, while recent underperformers are sold. It is important to know that with investments, **past performance is not indicative of future results**.

Herd mentality. There is a comfort in being part of a group. When others do something we are more comfortable doing the same. A recent example is the influx of money into mortgage-backed securities and risky loans, and the debacle that followed. Of course, history has shown that when the herd moves in one direction it may be time to consider going the other way. (See chapter 5, The Rebalancing Decision, for how to avoid this problem).

Fear of regret. We are often reluctant to make investment decisions for fear they will turn out badly. For example, have you ever left money sitting uninvested because you were afraid to enter the market at the wrong time? Our view is that **the right time to invest is when you have the money and the right time to sell is when you need the money.**

Affinity traps (Bernie Madoff, anyone?). Instead of doing our own research, how often do we make an investment simply because we have mutual ties to an organization, or because it was recommended by a respected friend or famous person?

Certainly, there are other emotions that are hazardous to our financial health if left unchecked. Many of us can relate to an observation made by the economic historian Charles Kindleberger, author of the classic *Manias, Panics and Crashes*: "There is nothing so disturbing to one's well-being and judgment as to see a friend get rich."

Market fluctuations cause us to continuously battle against our biases. We need *discipline* to counter these normal human tendencies. The right discipline begins with an understanding of how markets work. It establishes a process that allows us to focus our time and effort on those things we can control. This helps us achieve our investment goals more efficiently and with less worry.

It is very difficult to accomplish this on your own without a good steward in your corner. This is why we believe most investors who are serious about managing their wealth should seek the assistance of a professional. A qualified financial advisor should bring discipline and clarity to the investment process and help you avoid behavioral traps that can impede your ability to realize your financial goals.

If you agree with us, the question then becomes which type of advisor to choose: a *retail broker* or an *independent, fee-only advisor*.

Years ago, before the widespread availability of independent, fee-only advisors, retail brokers were the primary means of obtaining investment advice. Now you have a choice. There are significant differences between the two that you must understand.

RETAIL BROKERS

Retail brokers are commissioned agents compensated by their firm or a third party for selling you investment products. Traditionally known as stock brokers, today they call themselves Financial Advisors and Financial Consultants. **Despite the titles they put on their business cards, they should not be confused with independent, fee-only advisors.**

Retail brokers typically offer two different types of accounts — a "classic" brokerage account and an investment advisory account.

Brokerage Account

With a brokerage account your broker will act as an agent for his firm. In this capacity, **your broker's first duty is to his firm, not to you**, even though you are his customer. While he may offer the periodic stock tip or some occasional advice, that is incidental to his main business of generating trades and commissions.[1]

With this type of account, your broker is not held to the legal standards of the Investment Advisers Act of 1940, which requires that anyone who offers both investment advice and charges an asset-based or flat fee to register as an investment advisor. According to the law, advisors must disclose any conflicts of interest and put their clients' interests first. You do not get this protection with a brokerage account.

With a brokerage account, you should be aware of these potential conflicts and drawbacks inherent in the relationship:

Your broker is:

a. better compensated for generating more trades;

b. better compensated for selling certain investment products over others; and

c. limited to selling the investment products approved by his firm.

---

[1] Robert Barker, "Will the SEC Bless This Masquerade?" *Business Week,* August 5, 2002.

Investment Advisory Account

With an investment advisory or "managed account" your broker may offer many services such as financial planning and advice on the selection of investment managers and investment products — all for a single fee.

With managed accounts, your broker is held to the legal standards of the 1940 Advisers Act. He is therefore considered to have a fiduciary relationship with you and must disclose any conflicts of interest and put your interests first. While these advisory accounts eliminate much potential for abuse, there are drawbacks with this model as well.

For example, the broker is still limited to offering only his firm's menu of approved investment products. In addition, the investment managers or mutual funds he recommends to you may be paying his brokerage firm to be included as an approved investment for all its clients.

It also might be the case that the investments you have through your broker's current firm may not be transferrable to another firm. This could mean having to sell your investments, potentially triggering costly capital gains, to move your account to another firm, either to switch to a new broker or to follow your current broker when he moves to a new firm.

The Name Game and Changing Hat Tricks

It is important to keep in mind that regulators have done a poor job of policing the dozens of misleading titles that brokers often use. This means that you are on your own when it comes to asking the hard questions about whether they really work for you. Don't believe those glitzy ads that you see in the *Wall Street Journal* or on TV about how they work just for you.

To complicate things even more, not all brokers work for Wall Street firms, although they still face the same conflicts and incentives. Some brokers may call themselves independent because technically they are not employees of a Wall Street firm. Instead, they are independent contractors of a brokerage house that might even be based in your home town. There are some 5,000 such firms around the country with thousands of branch offices. To clear things up, simply ask if they are a *registered representative* — this is the technical term used by all brokers. If so, they are not truly independent.

Closely related to the name game is the *hat changing* issue when dealing with someone who is registered as an *advisor* and *broker*. While brokers are required to act in a fiduciary role when giving investment advice under the 1940 Advisers Act, they can "switch hats" and act as a salesperson when selling you other investment or retirement products. This can be a problem because, with any advice you receive, you'll need to ascertain whether it's for your benefit, or because they're getting a commission on the sale. In short, you need to be wary of a potential "bait and switch" problem caused by gaps in the law.

INDEPENDENT, FEE-ONLY ADVISORS

In contrast to brokers, **independent, fee-only advisors are always legally required to act as *fiduciaries* to their clients**. This means that they must put their clients' interests first. Also, independent, fee-only advisors should be more closely aligned with their clients because they are generally free from the conflicts, constraints, and pressures that brokers face.

Compensation

An independent advisor will generally calculate his fee as a percentage of the amount of money he is managing for you. Because of economies of scale, this percentage fee generally declines as your account size increases. Unlike a broker, whose fees are often buried in hard-to-read disclosure documents, an advisor's compensation is described in a straightforward, transparent fashion. Also, unlike a broker, an independent advisor only receives compensation from you. He does not receive payment from the investments he selects for you or commissions from moving your money back and forth between investments.

Custody of Your Assets

An independent, fee-only advisor should use a third-party custodian (a firm like Charles Schwab or Fidelity) to serve as the safe-keeper of your investments. These firms are responsible for ensuring that your money is in a separate account under your name with your advisor only having the limited authority to manage the account on your behalf. You receive regular statements, trade confirmations, and other information about your account directly from your custodian. **Under no circumstances should you work with any advisor that takes custody of your money himself.** This is how Bernie Madoff and others were able to steal from their clients.

We want to say again that **an advisor is a *fiduciary* who must put your interests ahead of his own**. Without the financial incentive to generate more trades or sell higher margin products, or the limitations of only having his firm's approved investment offerings, an advisor is free to use any money manager or type of investment product that he feels is best for you.

A capable advisor can help you stay disciplined and avoid the temptation to move money from security to security, market to market, or money manager to money manager — particularly at times when the potentially destructive emotions of fear or greed set in. Because independent, fee-only advisors are not spending their time thinking about how to generate additional revenue from your account, they have the capacity to help you with many other important financial decisions — such as retirement and estate planning, insurance questions, and whether to refinance your mortgage.

In our opinion, the difference is clear: **A broker is working for his firm. An independent fee-only advisor is working for you.**

HOW TO SELECT AN INDEPENDENT, FEE-ONLY ADVISOR

Finding the right independent, fee-only advisor for you is important. You don't want to hire an advisor only to later feel like you want to make a change. Getting the right person from the start will save you both emotionally and financially.

We have found that there are two areas of "fit" that are essential for having a long-term, successful relationship with an advisor:

1. **Investment philosophy.** There are many different philosophies and methods of managing investments and providing financial advice. After reading this book, you will have a clear sense of the investment approach that you feel is best. You want to find an advisor that shares your investment philosophy and thinks about investing and markets the same way that you do. Of course, you want your advisor to have — and be able to articulate well — a clear set of investment beliefs and methods. If he does not have a clearly defined view or cannot communicate it well, you should look for a different advisor.

2. **Personal connection and trust.** You will be establishing a close working relationship with your advisor — sharing important personal information (both financial and emotional) about yourself and your family. To do his job best, your advisor needs to know you well. In addition to the financial facts, he needs to understand your feelings about money, and your dreams and aspirations for the future. Do not hire an advisor if you don't feel comfortable sharing this information with him!

Some other things to consider as you interview potential advisors include:

Professional qualifications — An advisor who has earned one or more professional designations has demonstrated a commitment to education and professionalism, and at least reasonable proficiency in his field. Some common professional financial designations include: Certified Financial Planner (CFP), Chartered Financial Analyst (CFA), and Certified Public Accountant (CPA).

Education — As you might inquire about a potential employee's formal education, knowing where an advisor went to school and what he studied can help indicate his level of general intelligence, knowledge, and ability to problem-solve.

Experience — Financial advisors often have a variety of careers before they become advisors. Knowing an advisor's work history can help you evaluate his level of experience and relative success. You should be careful before engaging an advisor who is very new to the profession or has not demonstrated success in financial services or a related pursuit such as accounting.

Business structure — Advisory firms have a variety of organizational structures. Some advisors work as solo practitioners. Others work in small professional partnerships, and a few work in larger organizations with many employees and advisors. There are advantages and disadvantages of each structure, and you want to be sure you understand how a business is set up before you become a client.

Services offered — Some advisors only offer asset management while others offer a more complete set of services that usually includes personal financial planning (sometimes called wealth management). It can be helpful to work with an advisor who incorporates financial planning into his practice because investment decisions should be made only after considering one's overall financial situation.

Current clients — You should ask a potential advisor about the types of clients he works with and who he feels is his ideal client. You don't want to be an unusual client — it is better to fit well within an advisor's client base so that you benefit from his experiences with others like you.

CHAPTER 2

The
Asset Allocation
Decision

THE IMPACT OF VOLATILITY ON RETURNS

It is essential to have a good understanding of risk to make an informed decision regarding which general asset classes to include in your investment portfolio. Wall Street and the financial media often focus on an investment's potential return (how much you might make on the investment) rather than the risk you must take in order to achieve that return. An understanding of risk and the relationship between risk and return is necessary for any prudent long-term investor to make smart investment decisions.

For long-term investors there are two general types of investments that make up a portfolio:

1. **Equities (or stocks)** — are an ownership interest in a company. If the company does well, as a shareholder you should benefit from its rising stock price. The company might also pay a discretionary dividend to shareholders in the form of cash or more shares of stock. If the company does poorly, its stock price might go down, causing your shares to decline in value. There are many factors that can affect a company's stock price, many of which are completely

external to the company itself. In general, equity investments are considered *higher risk/higher expected return* investments.

2. **Fixed income (or bonds)** — are an I.O.U. or a loan to an entity such as the U.S. government, a state, or a company. Bonds are contractual obligations that usually involve interest payments paid by the borrower at regular intervals and, ultimately, the return of your initial investment at maturity date. Bonds are generally considered to be *lower risk/lower expected return* investments (especially high-quality, short-term bonds).

Financial economists have identified many types of investment risk, such as:

Credit Risk — the risk that a company's credit quality could wane and you, as a bondholder or creditor, could lose some or all of your investment.

Inflation Risk — your portfolio's real return (the return you get after deducting inflation) can be much less than its nominal (pre-inflation) return, especially over longer time periods. This is one of the most significant risks for long-term investors.

Maturity Risk — longer-term bonds have more risk (and price volatility) than shorter-term bonds. After all, if you lend me money for ten years, isn't that a riskier proposition than if you lend it to me for only one month?

Market Risk — this is the non-diversifiable risk inherent in any securities market. If you own a stock, the largest element of risk you are taking is that the stock market as a whole might go down. If it does, the market will likely take your stock down with it.

There are many other types of risk as well. **The common denominator in all measures of risk is the uncertainty of future results.**

In the investment world, the most widely used measure of risk is *standard deviation*, which is a statistical measure of the degree to which numbers in a series (such as the annual returns of an investment) differ from their average. Under normal

"October is one of the peculiarly dangerous months to speculate in stocks. The others are July, January, September, April, November, May, March, June, December, August and February." — MARK TWAIN

circumstances, about two-thirds of the numbers will fall within one standard deviation of the mean (average).

One way to think about this concept is to consider two different investments with different risk and return characteristics. For example, Fund A has an expected average return of four percent with an expected standard deviation of two percent. This means that about two-thirds of the time this investment is expected to return between two percent and six percent (plus or minus two percent). Fund B, on the other hand, has a higher expected average return of 10 percent, but also has a higher expected standard deviation of 20 percent, meaning that about two-thirds of the time Fund B should return between 30 percent and -10 percent (plus or minus 20 percent).

Clearly an investment in Fund B would entail more risk (or uncertainty of future return) than Fund A. After all, an investor in Fund B who needed to raise cash at an inopportune time would suffer more when that fund had declined 10 percent versus the investor in Fund A who might only be down two percent under similar adverse conditions.

A related point has to do with the growth of money over time. Consider Figure 2-1 that shows two hypothetical portfolios — a low volatility portfolio and a high volatility portfolio. Each portfolio has the same average rate of return of 10 percent per year. However, the low volatility portfolio has steadier returns, and the high volatility portfolio has more ups and downs.

The fact that the low volatility portfolio ends up with more wealth may be surprising to many, but it is a mathematical certainty. This is because ending wealth is determined by the compound return, not the average return. It's like the children's story of the tortoise and the hare. The hare races like crazy but is out of control, and ultimately the tortoise wins the race.

The impact of volatility on returns becomes more pronounced over time and with a greater difference in standard deviation. Remember that a portfolio that is down 50 percent requires a 100 percent appreciation just to get back to even. On the other hand, a portfolio that is down only 8.0 percent requires a recovery of just 8.7 percent to make up that loss. This is because the greater the loss, the smaller the base upon which your earnings can compound.

Figure 2-1 The Impact Of Volatility On Returns

Year	Low Volatility Growth of $100,000	Annual Return	High Volatility Growth of $100,000	Annual Return
1	$110,000	10.0%	$134,000	34.0%
2	$115,500	5.0%	$121,940	-9.0%
3	$131,670	14.0%	$153,644	26.0%
4	$143,520	9.0%	$129,061	-16.0%
5	$162,178	13.0%	$169,070	31.0%
6	$165,421	2.0%	$167,380	-1.0%
7	$185,272	12.0%	$197,508	18.0%
8	$214,916	16.0%	$173,807	-12.0%
9	$227,811	6.0%	$210,306	21.0%
10	$257,426	13.0%	$227,313	8.0%
Average Return		10.0%		10.0%
Compound Return		9.9%		8.5%
Standard Deviation		4.5%		18.6%

Hypothetical portfolios for illustrative purposes only. Diversification does not assure a profit or protect against a loss.

RISK AND RETURN ARE RELATED

Although Wall Street and the media encourage us to believe that we can find a "free lunch" or a market pricing error, these opportunities are very difficult to exploit. In other words, **there are no *low risk/high expected return* investments**.

Here's why: if an investment offered a disproportionately high return for the risk it involved, word would spread and others would try to capitalize on it. This additional demand would result in the price of the investment being driven up to the point where its expected return is commensurate with other investments of similar risk.

This is how free markets work. Each day the prices of tens of thousands of publicly traded stocks and bonds around the world continuously adjust to reflect new information or developments.

The long-term relationship between risk and return is very clearly illustrated in the revolutionary work done by Roger Ibbotson and Rex Sinquefield in the 1970s. Their studies of historical capital market returns give us the intellectual foundation for favoring one asset class over another.

An asset class is a group of similar investment securities that share common, and objectively defined, risk and return characteristics. Figure 2-2 extends the original work by Ibbotson and Sinquefield through the end of 2009. It shows the comparative returns and growth of a dollar invested in four major asset classes and inflation since 1926.

Figure 2-2 U.S. Capital Market Returns

Growth of $1: January 1, 1926 to December 31, 2009

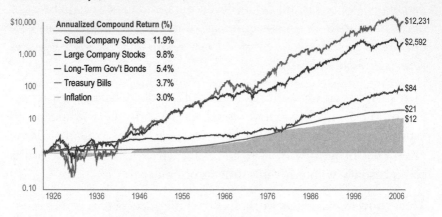

For illustrative purposes only. All investments involve risk, including loss of principal. Past performance is not indicative of future results. Indices are unmanaged baskets of securities in which investors cannot directly invest. Small company stocks are represented by the CRSP 9-10 Index; Large Company Stocks by the Standard & Poor's 500 Index; Long-Term Government Bonds by the 20-Year U.S. Government Bond; Treasury Bills by the 30-day U.S. Treasury Bill.

Small vs. Large Companies

The growth lines in the figure above underscore how risk and return are related. For example, **small company stocks are riskier than large company stocks, and have therefore delivered a higher return**. Why? Assume you are a banker considering making a loan to a very small company as well as a big company like General Electric. To which would you charge a higher interest rate? The small company, of course, because it is more risky and has a greater likelihood of defaulting on the loan.

Equity investors view risk in a similar way. They also demand a higher rate of return from smaller companies. The fact that small company stocks have outperformed large company stocks represents a dimension of risk known as the *size effect*. **This higher return is a reward for taking greater risk** in a properly functioning free capital market.

Both small and large company stocks are riskier than bonds, especially bonds issued by the most creditworthy borrower of all, the U.S. treasury. So it is no surprise that large and small company stocks have returned more than long-term government bonds, which, in turn, have returned more than treasury bills (which are less risky due to their shorter maturities).

Of course, in any given year treasury bills could outperform stocks, as a close look at Figure 2-2 will demonstrate. However, as long-term investors we should look beyond these short-term performance variations. Historical data and investment theory strongly suggest that a risk and return hierarchy should prevail over time.

Value vs. Growth Companies

The other important dimension of risk in the equity markets is referred to as the *value effect*. **Value stocks have low stock prices relative to their underlying accounting measures such as book value, sales and earnings.** These are distressed companies and may have poor earnings growth or bleak prospects for the future. In contrast, a *growth* stock is a very healthy company that is highly profitable and growing fast. **Growth stocks have high stock prices relative to their underlying accounting measures.**

At the time of this writing, many large bank stocks are considered value stocks. They have significant assets, but they also have notable financial problems. Equity investors demand a higher return from large banking stocks today given their greater risk.

Figure 2-3 shows the historical return advantage of small stocks over large, and value stocks over growth. Small stocks in the U.S. since 1926 have appreciated about two percent per year more than large stocks, and large value stocks have outperformed large growth stocks by more than one percent.

Figure 2-3 Size and Value Effects

January 1, 1973 to December 31, 2009

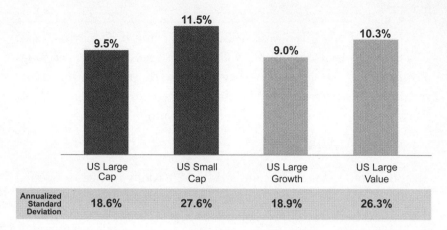

	US Large Cap	US Small Cap	US Large Growth	US Large Value
	9.5%	11.5%	9.0%	10.3%
Annualized Standard Deviation	18.6%	27.6%	18.9%	26.3%

For illustrative purposes only. All investments involve risk, including loss of principal. Past performance is not indicative of future results. Indices are unmanaged baskets of securities in which investors cannot directly invest. Assumes reinvestment of income and no transaction costs or taxes. Standard deviation is a statistical measurement of how far the return of a security (or index) moves above or below its average value. The greater the standard deviation, the riskier an investment is considered to be. U.S. large-cap stocks are represented by the CRSP Deciles 1-5 Index, U.S. small-cap stocks by the CRSP Deciles 6-10 Index, U.S. large growth stocks by the Fama-French U.S. Large Growth Index, U.S. large value stocks by the Fama-French U.S. Large Value Index. Full descriptions of indices used above are located in the Sources and Descriptions of Data section in this book.

Figure 2-4 shows an easy way to visualize the two main factors that drive the long-term investment returns of stocks: *company size* and *valuation*. A portfolio more heavily weighted to small and value stocks has a higher expected long-term return.

Where your overall equity portfolio is positioned on this map will be far more important in determining your investment returns than which individual stocks you pick or which particular money managers or mutual funds you use!

Figure 2-4

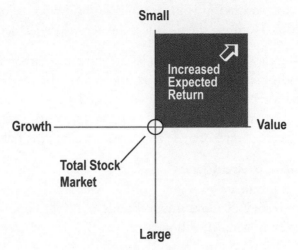

Cross Section of Expected Stock Returns, Fama, E. F. and French, K. R., *Journal of Finance 47* (1992)

Long-term investors who can withstand the greater short-term volatility of riskier asset classes should be rewarded over time with higher returns. Remember, risk and return are related!

THE ASSET ALLOCATION DECISION

What will be the primary determinant of your investment performance? Wall Street brokers and the financial press would have you believe that investment results are mostly determined by how successful you are at: (1) *timing* when to get in and out of the market, (2) *picking* the right individual stocks and bonds to own, or (3) *finding* the next top-performing manager or mutual fund (or all of the above).

Wrong! Research shows that these factors make a negative contribution to the total return level of a diversified portfolio.[1] For the most part, these activities waste your time, cost you money, and reduce your return.

It is important to understand that **the primary driver of investment returns is risk**, specifically the riskiness of (and the relationship between)

[1] Xiong, J. X., Ibbotson, R. G., Idzorek, T. M. and Chen, P., 2010. "The Equal Importance of Asset Allocation and Active Management," *Financial Analysts' Journal*, March/April.

the asset classes you use in your portfolio and how you allocate your investment dollars among them. This is the *asset allocation* decision.

Again, an asset class is a group of similar investment securities that share common and objectively defined risk and return characteristics. The most general asset classes are cash, stocks, and bonds. Within these broad categories are specific asset classes that more narrowly capture certain risk factors. Some of these asset classes include the following:

Fixed Income Asset Classes
Cash Equivalents
Short-Term U.S. Government Bonds
Short-Term Municipal Bonds
High-Quality, Short-Term Corporate Bonds
High-Quality, Short-Term Global Bonds

Equity Asset Classes
U.S. Large Stocks
U.S. Large Value Stocks
U.S. Small Stocks
U.S. Small Value Stocks
International Large Stocks
International Large Value Stocks
International Small Stocks
International Small Value Stocks
Emerging Markets Stocks (Large, Small, and Value)
Real Estate Stocks (Domestic and International)

You should approach this decision first by focusing on your desired mix of cash, bonds, and stocks. **This is the single most important investment decision you will make!**

Cash

As a guideline, the percentage of assets invested in cash equivalents — which are safe, easily accessible, short-term investments such as treasury bills, bank CDs, and money market funds (*lowest risk/least return*) — should be based on how quickly you might need to access these funds. Certainly, any money required in less than one year should be invested in cash equivalents.

Bonds (*lower risk/lower return*) **and Stocks** (*higher risk/higher return*)

Since stocks are riskier than bonds, it follows that they should provide higher returns in the long run. Bonds, therefore, should be viewed as a tool for reducing the volatility of your portfolio. As such, we recommend that you restrict your bond holdings to higher quality and shorter maturity issues, such as short-term U.S. treasuries, government agencies, and the high-quality corporate bonds. These are the safest and least volatile fixed income asset classes.

There are two reasons we recommend that you include bonds in your mix:

1. **Your emotional tolerance for risk.** There will be years when stocks go down 20 percent, 30 percent, or more. It can be difficult to withstand such short-term pain and you want to be sure that you do not set yourself up for failure. Studies have shown that investors tend to panic and sell at or near the bottom of market decline, causing them to miss the subsequent recovery. For example, in 1973 and 1974 a globally diversified portfolio of stocks would have been down about 19 percent and 23 percent, respectively. Investors who panicked and sold likely missed the subsequent recovery in 1975 and 1976 when the same portfolio was up approximately 41 percent and 28 percent, respectively.

   A similar story unfolded after the market declines of 2000-2002, and 2008. Investors should understand their emotional ability to "stomach" occasional down years in equities. With a portfolio that is properly allocated to match your risk tolerance, you will be more likely to maintain your investment discipline and enjoy better investment returns over the long term.

2. Your Age. A younger investor is a better candidate for an asset mix more heavily weighted toward equities. He will most likely not need to withdraw money from his investment portfolio for decades, his future earning capacity is his greatest asset, and he should be better able to emotionally withstand the short-term ups and downs of the market. In contrast, a retiree whose earning capacity is limited and who is withdrawing part of his portfolio each year for living expenses should not be too exposed to stocks and a potential extended stock market downturn. He may want to lessen the volatility of his portfolio with more exposure to bonds.

Figure 2-5 shows the historical returns and risk relationships of hypothetical balanced portfolios with different stock and bond allocations for the period January 1, 1973 to December 31, 2009. This period contains three of the worst bear markets in history, as well as one of the most sustained bull markets. The specific asset classes used to build these portfolios and their weightings appear in the appendix of this book.

Figure 2-5 Summary Statistics

January 1, 1973 to December 31, 2009

	HYPOTHETICAL PORTFOLIOS					
	Fixed	Defensive	Conservative	Moderate	Aggressive	Equity
Equity	0%	20%	40%	60%	80%	100%
Fixed Income	100%	80%	60%	40%	20%	0%
Annualized Return (%) 1973-2009	7.2	8.8	10.2	11.5	12.5	13.3
Annualized Standard Deviation (%) 1973-2009	2.5	3.9	6.6	9.7	12.8	16.1
Growth of $1 1973-2009	$12.99	$22.73	$36.96	$55.95	$78.72	$102.46

Assumes annual rebalancing. Annualized standard deviation is calculated from monthly data. Results are based on performance of indices with model/back-tested asset allocations. The performance was achieved with the benefit of hindsight; it does not represent actual investment strategies. The model's performance does not reflect advisory fees or other expenses associated with the management of an actual portfolio. There are limitations inherent in model allocations. In particular, model performance may not reflect the impact that economic and market factors may have had on the advisor's decision making if the advisor were actually managing client money. Past performance is no guarantee of future results.

CHAPTER 3

The Diversification Decision

Once you and your advisor have decided on the general asset class mix of stocks, bonds, and cash that is right for you, it is time to focus on the specific asset class building blocks to include in your portfolio. While many people understand the idea of "not putting all your eggs in one basket," most do not understand the concept of *effective diversification*.

To illustrate, here is a typical situation that we saw during the technology bubble of the late 1990s. A technology executive, in an effort to diversify his large holding of one technology company, bought 10 other technology companies. He thought he was diversifying and was smart to stay with an industry he knew well. Unfortunately, when technology stocks crashed as a group (because they share many common risk factors) his wealth was severely damaged.

The true benefits of diversification are realized when an investor considers the relationship of each asset class to that of every other asset class in his portfolio. It turns out that some asset classes tend to increase in value when others go down (or at least they don't go down as much). Asset classes that tend to move in tandem, such as companies in the same industry group or those that share similar risk factors, are said to be *positively correlated*.

Assets that move independently are *uncorrelated*, and those that move inversely are called *negatively correlated*.

Figure 3-1 illustrates the benefit of blending two hypothetical asset classes that are negatively correlated. Asset A has different risk and return characteristics than asset B and, therefore, their prices move in opposite directions (when A declines then B rises, and vice versa).

The line labeled AB that runs down the center illustrates a blended portfolio that holds both of these assets equally. **The blended portfolio has lower volatility (i.e., lower standard deviation) than either individual asset.**

This is an important component of what financial economists call *Modern Portfolio Theory*. The concept was introduced in 1952 by the Nobel Laureate economist Harry Markowitz.[1] Markowitz first described this idea using individual stocks, but the concept works equally well with mutual funds or entire asset classes.

Figure 3-1

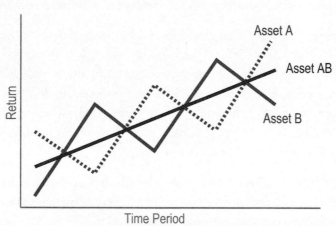

For illustrative purposes only. Diversification does not assure a profit and does not protect against loss in declining markets.

---

[1] Markowitz, H., 1952, Portfolio Selection, *Journal of Finance* 7, 77-91

This concept underscores another very important tenet of investing: **focus on the performance of your portfolio as a whole, rather than the returns of its individual components**. Do not be discouraged that in any given period some asset classes will not do as well as others.

Domestic Stocks

As a U.S. investor, which specific asset classes should be included in your mix? While this important topic should lend itself to a much broader discussion with your advisor, a reasonable place to start would be to allocate some of your money to domestic large cap stocks, such as the stocks included in the S&P 500 index. After all, these 500 companies account for about 70% of the market capitalization of the entire U.S. stock market.

You can then work with your advisor to identify other domestic equity asset classes that would complement and provide diversification benefits to U.S. large company stocks. We recommend including exposure to U.S. small cap and value stocks, as they can increase your portfolio's expected return and broaden its diversification. Likewise, real estate investment trusts can serve as a useful diversifier when blended with traditional equity asset classes.

International Stocks

No discussion about investing would be complete without mentioning the benefits of diversifying internationally. Many investors are surprised to discover that the U.S. stock market currently accounts for less than half of the market value of the world's equity markets. There are many investment and diversification opportunities outside our borders. In addition, with the advances in technology, professional money managers now have up-to-the-minute information about developments in countries all over the world, and the ability to move billions from market to market nearly instantaneously. As a result, the long-term expected returns of international asset classes are similar to those of comparable domestic asset classes.

In the short run, the performance of international asset classes can be very different from domestic asset classes. Sometimes international outperforms the U.S., and sometimes the U.S. does better. This is due largely to countries and regions being at different points in their economic cycles, having fluctuating exchange rates, and exercising independent fiscal and monetary policies.

The diversification benefits of international investing are stronger when you include international small-cap and value stocks, as well as emerging market securities (stocks of companies in developing countries). Stocks of these developing countries are especially valuable for diversification because their prices tend to be more closely related to their local economies than to the global economy. By way of contrast, a large international company such as Nestle has operations all over the world, and thus is likely to have a higher correlation with other large companies in the U.S. and abroad.

Domestic Bonds

Remember that the role of fixed income is to reduce the overall volatility of your portfolio. When including bonds in your mix, we recommend using higher quality issues (bonds with higher credit ratings) and those with shorter maturities (less than five years) reduce risk most effectively. These types of bonds are safer, more liquid, and less volatile.

International Bonds

Like international stocks, international bonds can be excellent diversifiers for your portfolio. As with domestic fixed income, consider using shorter maturities and higher-quality issues. An international bond portfolio that blends U.S. bonds with those from other developed countries can have lower risk and greater expected returns than a comparable all-U.S. bond portfolio.

USE ASSET CLASSES

With the help of today's sophisticated computer programs, an advisor can access the historical risk and return data of different asset classes and construct a portfolio that maximizes expected returns for any given level of risk. Figure 3-2 demonstrates this concept. Higher risk/return portfolios usually have greater percentages in stocks.

Notice that the risk level reduces as the initial stock market exposure (up to about 20 percent) is added to the 100 percent bond portfolio. This is caused by the diversification benefits available from adding riskier assets that do not move in perfect unison with the other assets in your portfolio.

It's up to you and your advisor to determine how much risk is appropriate for you.

Figure 3-2 Portfolio Risk and Return

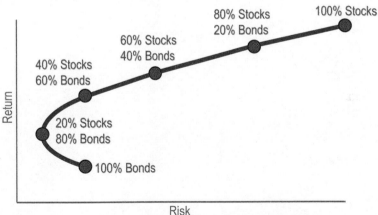

Based on historical information and assumptions about the future. Not intended to project future performance results. Chart for illustrative purposes only.

CHAPTER 4

The
Active versus Passive
Decision

ACTIVE INVESTING

Active managers attempt to "beat the market" (or their relevant benchmarks) through a variety of techniques such as stock picking and market timing. In contrast, passive managers avoid subjective forecasts, take a longer-term view, and work to deliver market-like returns.

The Efficient Markets Hypothesis asserts that **no investor will consistently beat the market over long periods except by chance**. Active managers test this hypothesis every day through their efforts to outperform their benchmarks and deliver superior risk-adjusted returns. The preponderance of evidence shows that their efforts are unsuccessful.

Figure 4-1 shows the percentage of actively managed equity mutual funds that failed to outperform their respective benchmarks for the five-year period ending December 31, 2009. The message here is that **most funds failed to beat their respective benchmarks**. (If international small-cap managers had been correctly compared to an index that included emerging markets, the rate of underperformance would rise to the 70 to 80 percent range, which is in line with the other categories.)

Figure 4-1 Active Managers Failing to Beat Their Benchmark (%)

January 1, 2005 – December 31, 2009

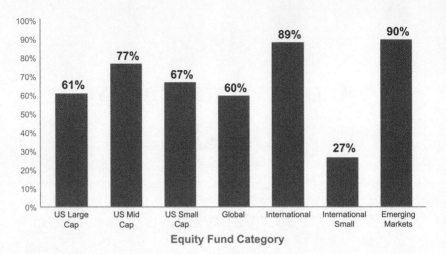

Source: Standard & Poor's Indices Versus Active Funds Scorecard, March 30, 2010. Indicies used for comparison: US Large Cap—S&P 500 Index, US Mid Cap—S&P Mid Cap 400 Index, US Small Cap—S&P Small Cap Index, Global Funds— S&P Global 1200 Index, International—S&P 700 Index, International Small—S&P Developed ex.-US Small Cap Index, Emerging Markets—S&P IFCI Composite. Data for the SPIVA study is from the CRSP Survior-Bias-Free US Mutual Fund Database. Results are net of fees and expenses. Indices are not available for direct investment.

Active managers attempt to outperform the market (or a benchmark index) by assembling a portfolio that is different from the market. Active managers think they can beat the market through superior analysis and research. Sometimes, these managers consider fundamental factors such as accounting data or economic statistics. Others will perform technical analysis using charts and graphs of historical prices, trading volume, or other indicators, believing these are predictive of future price movements.

For the most part, in an attempt to beat their benchmarks, active managers will make concentrated bets by holding only those securities they think will be the top performers and rejecting the rest. This approach, of course, comes at the expense of diversification. It also makes it difficult to use active strategies in a portfolio to reliably capture the returns of a target asset class or control a portfolio's overall allocation.

Studies show that **the returns of active managers can be very different from their benchmarks, and their portfolios often overlap across multiple asset classes.**

There are two primary ways that active managers try to beat the market: (1) *Market timing,* and (2) *Security selection.*

Market timers attempt to predict the future direction of market prices and place a bet accordingly. Because **no one can reliably predict the future, it should come as no surprise that the overwhelming evidence suggests market timing is a losing proposition.**

Another reason it is so hard to time markets is that **markets tend to have bursts of large gains (or losses) that are concentrated in a relatively small number of trading days.** Figure 4-2 shows that if an investor misses just a few of the best performing trading days, he loses a large percentage of the market's total returns. We believe it is impossible to predict ahead of time when the best (or worst) days will occur.

Figure 4-2 Performance of the S&P 500 Index

Daily: January 1, 1970 – December 31, 2009

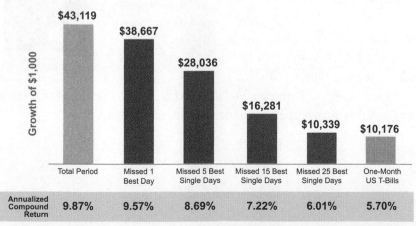

	Total Period	Missed 1 Best Day	Missed 5 Best Single Days	Missed 15 Best Single Days	Missed 25 Best Single Days	One-Month US T-Bills
Annualized Compound Return	9.87%	9.57%	8.69%	7.22%	6.01%	5.70%

Data for January 1970-August 2009 provided by CRSP. Data for September 2008-December 2009 provided by Bloomberg. S&P data provided by Standard & Poor's Index Services Group. CRSP data provided by the Center for Research in Security Prices, University of Chicago. Treasury bills data © Stocks, Bonds, Bills, and Inflation Yearbook™, Ibbotson Associates, Chicago. Indices are not available for direct investment. Performance does not reflect the expenses associated with the management of an actual portfolio. Past performance is not a guarantee of future results. There is always a risk an investor will lose money.

The other active management technique is *security selection* (or stock picking). This involves attempting to identify securities that are mispriced by the market with the hope that the pricing error will soon correct itself and the securities will outperform. In Wall Street parlance, an active manager considers a security to be either undervalued, overvalued, or fairly valued. Active managers buy the securities they think are undervalued (the potential "winners") and sell those they think are overvalued (the potential "losers").

You should know that whenever you buy or sell a security, you are making a bet. You are trading against the view of many market participants who may have better information than you do. When markets are working properly, all known information is reflected in market prices, so your bet has about a 50% chance of beating the market (and less after costs are taken into account).

Again, Wall Street and the media have a vested interest in leading us to believe that we can beat the market if we are smarter and harder-working than others. Yet, through today's technological advances, new information is readily available and becomes almost instantly

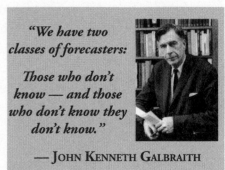

"We have two classes of forecasters:

Those who don't know — and those who don't know they don't know."

— JOHN KENNETH GALBRAITH

reflected in securities prices. **Markets work because no single investor can reliably profit at the expense of other investors.**

The idea that prices reflect all the knowledge and expectations of investors is known in academic circles as the Efficient Markets Hypothesis, which was developed by Professor Eugene Fama of the University of Chicago Booth School of Business.[1]

---

[1] Fama, E.F., 1965, "The Behavior of Stock-Market Prices," The *Journal of Business*, Vol. 38, No. 1 pp. 34-105

The Efficient Markets Hypothesis is sometimes misinterpreted as meaning that market prices are always correct. This is not the case. A properly functioning market may get prices wrong for a time, but it does so randomly and unpredictably such that no investor can systematically outperform other investors, or the market as a whole.

Finding the Winning Managers

Still, many investors want to believe that they will be able to beat the market if they can identify a smarter, harder-working, and more talented manager — a Roger Federer or Michael Jordan of money management. Of course, it is easy to find a top performer after the fact. They are then held out as "geniuses" by the media. But **how do you identify tomorrow's top managers *before* they have their run of good performance?**

The most common method is by examining past performance, the theory being that good past performance must mean good future performance. Financial magazines like *Forbes*, and rating services such as Morningstar, love to publish this data as these are some of their best selling issues. Mutual fund companies are also quick to advertise their best performing "hot funds" because this attracts new money from investors. Despite all of this activity, **there is little evidence to suggest that past performance is indicative of future performance**.

PASSIVE INVESTING

A more sensible approach to investing is passive investing. This is based on the belief that markets are efficient and extremely difficult to beat, especially after costs. Passive managers seek to deliver the returns of an asset class or sector of the market. They do this by investing very broadly in all, or a large portion of, the securities of a target asset class.

The best known (but not the only) method of passive investing is called *indexing*, which involves a manager purchasing all of the securities in a benchmark index in the exact proportions as the index. The manager then tracks (or replicates) the results of that benchmark, index less any operating costs. The most popular benchmark index is the S&P 500, which is comprised of 500 U.S. large cap stocks that currently make up about 70 percent of the market capitalization of the U.S. stock market.

Cash Drag

Because active managers are always looking for the next winner, they tend to keep more cash on hand so they can move quickly when the next (perceived) great investment opportunity arises. Since the return on short-term cash investments is generally much less than that of riskier asset classes like equities, holding these higher cash levels can end up reducing an active manager's returns. Passive managers are more fully invested, which means that more of your money is working for you all the time.

Consistency

Another advantage of passive investing is that you and your advisor can select a group of asset classes that work well together like the efficient building blocks of a portfolio. Done correctly, the building blocks will have few securities in common (called cross-holdings) and the risk and return profiles of each will be unique.

Sometimes an active manager will change his investment style in an attempt to beat his benchmark. For example, a large cap value manager may suddenly start purchasing large growth stocks if he feels that large growth stocks are about to take off. This "*style drift*" can be problematic, especially if you already have a large growth fund in your portfolio. In this case, you would now have overlapping risk and less diversification. **Trying to build a portfolio using active managers causes you to lose control of the diversification decision.**

Costs Matter

One explanation for the underperformance of active management was set forth by Nobel Laureate William Sharpe of Stanford University.

Sharpe ingeniously pointed out that, as a group, **active managers must always underperform passive managers.**[2] This is because investors as a whole can earn no more than the total return of the market (there is only so much juice in an orange). Since active managers' costs are higher — they pay more for trading and research — it follows that the return after costs from active managers as a group must be lower than that of passive managers.

This holds true for every asset class, even supposedly less-efficient ones like small-cap and emerging markets, where it is often said that active managers have an edge because information is less available. Sharpe's observation confirms that because of their higher costs in these markets, active managers should collectively underperform by more than in larger, more widely traded markets — the opposite of conventional wisdom.

The higher costs of active management can be broken down into three categories:

1. **Higher manager expenses.** It is more costly for an active manager to employ high-priced research analysts, technicians, and economists, all of whom are searching for the next great investment idea. Other active management costs include fund marketing and sales costs, such as 12b-1 fees and loads, to attract money from investors or to get Wall Street brokers to sell their funds. The expense differential between active and passive approaches to investing can exceed one percent per year.

2. **Increased turnover.** As active managers try to provide superior returns, they tend to trade more often and more aggressively than passive managers. This usually means paying greater brokerage commissions, which are passed on to shareholders in the form of reduced returns. It also means that market-impact costs can increase dramatically. When an active manager is motivated to

---

[2] Sharpe, W. F., 1991. "The Arithmetic of Active Management," *Financial Analysts' Journal,* Jan/Feb.

buy or sell, he may have to pay up significantly in order to execute the transaction quickly or in large volume (think of a motivated buyer or seller in real estate).

These higher market-impact costs are more prevalent in less liquid areas of the market such as small cap and emerging markets stocks. It is not uncommon for turnover in actively managed funds to exceed that of index funds by four times or more. The extra trading costs for active management can exceed one percent per year.

3. **Greater tax exposure.** Given that active managers trade more often, it follows that taxable investors will incur accelerated capital gains as a result. Remember, if your mutual fund sells a security for a gain, that profit may be passed on to you as a taxable distribution. For securities held longer than one year, you would pay the long-term capital gains rate, while short-term capital gains would apply for securities held less than one year. The additional taxes due to accelerated capital gains generated by active managers may exceed one percent per year.

It is important to understand that of these three categories, typically **only manager expenses are disclosed to investors**. These are usually expressed as a percentage of net asset value in the case of a mutual fund, and is called the operating expense of the fund. For actively managed equity funds, the average operating expense ratio is around 1.3 percent per year.[3] Passive funds, on the other hand, can cost much less than 0.5 percent.[4]

If the additional costs of active management run roughly two to three percent annually, then the active manager clearly faces a huge hurdle just to match the results of a passive alternative such as an index fund.

Figure 4-3 compares the ending value of a hypothetical investment (growing at a rate of eight percent per year before fees) at various rates

---

[3] Lipper Analytical Services, "Fund Expenses: A Transatlantic Study," September 2009
[4] Expense information about a particular mutual fund can be found in the Statement of Additional Information and the fund's prospectus.

of annual investment expenses. Notice how every incremental percent in costs can add up and reduce your long-term ending wealth.

Pay attention to the costs you pay!

Figure 4-3 Costs Matter

Growth of $1 Million: 8% Gross Return for 30 Years

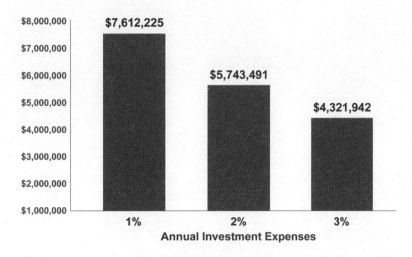

Assumes eight percent return before costs and no taxes paid. Net initial investment of $1 million. For Illustrative purposes only.

CHAPTER 5

The Rebalancing Decision

With a passive approach to investing using asset classes as your primary vehicles, there will be times when a minor adjustment to your portfolio's allocations will be beneficial. This change should not be based on a forecast, but rather on the fact that your portfolio has drifted away from its original asset class percentages and needs to be put back in line with its targets. This is called *rebalancing*.

For example, if equity markets enjoy a period of strong returns, it is possible that a 60-40 stock/bond portfolio could drift to a 70-30 mix. Left alone, your portfolio will have a higher risk level at what could turn out to be a market high point. By rebalancing back to the 60-40 mix you started with, you can maintain your desired level of risk and expected return.

In this example, rebalancing could be accomplished by either adding new money to your portfolio and investing in fixed income, withdrawing money from equities outright (perhaps for living expenses), or by selling some of the equities and reinvesting the proceeds into fixed income to bring the mix back to 60-40.

Psychologically, rebalancing is counter-intuitive and difficult for many investors. You might say to your advisor, "You really want me to sell my winners and buy more of those losers that haven't done anything for me in years? Are you crazy?"

We think this way because our intuition tells us to follow trends. We want to buy more of what has done well recently and sell what has done poorly. This can cause us to buy high and sell low — the opposite of what we should do. **Rebalancing is an automatic way to buy low and sell high, without your emotions getting in your way.**

Rebalancing Methods

It is important to note that rebalancing can be done in different ways. Some advisors prefer to rebalance on a fixed timetable, say at the same time each quarter. Others might review your portfolio on a fixed schedule, but only place trades if they identify one or more positions that are far enough out of alignment that rebalancing is necessary.

It is also possible to selectively place rebalancing trades only in certain types of accounts, like tax-deferred accounts, so that the tax ramifications of trading are reduced or deferred. Be sure to check with your advisor to determine his preferred method of rebalancing.

The Benefits of Rebalancing

An important benefit of rebalancing comes from keeping the allocation of your assets in line with your allocation targets, which allows you to maintain your chosen level of risk. You carefully selected your risk level based on your risk tolerance, time horizon, and other important factors. You don't want to allow market movements to haphazardly cause changes in your portfolio's risk level. You want to control this yourself and only change it when it makes sense to do so based on your long-term financial planning (and changes to that plan that may occur over time). For example, most people will want to gradually reduce their portfolio risk as they get older by reducing the percentage of money they have in stocks.

Rebalancing can also add value by managing the normal, yet unpredictable, market fluctuations that occur. For example, periods of high returns for an asset class are often followed by periods of low returns. By systematically selling asset classes when they are above their target weight, and buying them when they are below, you can best position your portfolio to maintain your desired amount of risk and acheive your desired rate of return.

To see how this might work, consider the example in figure 5-1. We have created two hypothetical portfolios with target allocations to the following asset classes from 1990 to 2009:[1]

15% U.S. Large Growth Stocks

15% U.S. Large Value Stocks

10% U.S. Small Growth Stocks

10% U.S. Small Value Stocks

10% Int'l Large Growth Stocks

10% Int'l Large Value Stocks

30% Long-Term Government Bonds

One portfolio is rebalanced back to its target percentages each year while the second is left to drift and is never rebalanced. As you might expect, the returns of the rebalanced portfolio were less volatile. This is because the rebalanced portfolio's allocations are maintained at their targets, whereas the allocations of the drifting portfolio increase over time to the riskier asset classes.

Some might be surprised that the rebalanced portfolio had higher average returns of 0.88 percent per year. This is not insignificant, as figure 5-1

---

[1] U.S. Large Growth Stocks represented by the Fama-French U.S. Large Growth Index, U.S. Large Value Stocks represented by the Fama-French U.S. Large Value Index, U.S. Small Growth Stocks represented by the Fama-French U.S. Small Growth Index, U.S. Small Value Stocks represented by the Fama-French U.S. Small Value Index, Int'l Large Growth Stocks represented by the MSCI EAFE Index, Int'l Large Value Stocks represented by the Fama-French Int'l Large Value Index, Long-Term Government Bonds represented by the Long-Term Government Bond Index. See the Sources and Descriptions of Data for complete information about these indicies.

illustrates. The reason for the higher returns? The rebalanced portfolio didn't decline as much during bad periods because it was kept in line with its target allocations and therefore didn't accumulate too much in asset classes that declined the most.

Figure 5-1 Growth of $1

January 1, 1990 to December 31, 2009

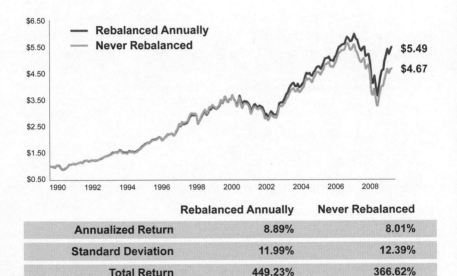

	Rebalanced Annually	Never Rebalanced
Annualized Return	8.89%	8.01%
Standard Deviation	11.99%	12.39%
Total Return	449.23%	366.62%

This is a hypothetical portfolio that may not be suitable for all investors. It reflects index returns without fees and expenses. It may not reflect the impact material economic and market factors might have had on decision making if clients' assets were actually being managed at that time. Assumes dividend and capital gain reinvestment. Asset allocation models may not be suitable for all investors. Performance results do not represent actual trading, but were achieved using backtesting with the benefit of hindsight. Actual results may vary. Indices are not available for direct investment.

Conclusions

CHAPTER 6

Compared

to

What?

We all want to know how our investments are doing. Unfortunately, Wall Street and the financial press do not have the incentives or the tools to give us an effective gauge of our results. We therefore often end up basing our opinions on how our friends or neighbors are doing, or on a media report.

Here is the right way to think about this:

The most common benchmark for U.S. stock market investors is the S&P 500 index, which most people refer to as *the market*. While the S&P 500 is currently comprised of about 70% of the market capitalization of the U.S. stock market, it still represents only one specific asset class: domestic large company stocks. It is often inappropriately used as a benchmark for investors whose portfolios have very different risk characteristics.

For example, balanced portfolios like the ones we discuss in this book include numerous other asset classes, each with different risk and return characteristics than the S&P 500. Knowing that risk and return are related, it should come as no surprise that the long-term expected return of the S&P 500 is lower than that of the total stock market and many other equity asset classes such as small-cap and value stocks. After all, the largest companies like those in the S&P 500 are generally considered to be the safest. They should be priced to have lower expected returns. This means **the S&P 500 index is a good benchmark for you ONLY if your portfolio contains domestic large company stocks and no others**.

Since your balanced portfolio has many different asset classes, the S&P 500 (or any other single asset class benchmark) is not a good benchmark to use. Given the highly diversified nature of your portfolio, what benchmark should you use?

Your advisor should be able to find at least one relevant benchmark for each asset class in your portfolio. **An appropriate benchmark is one that has similar risk characteristics to its target asset class.** For your stocks, the benchmarks should have the same *size* and *value* characteristics as the asset classes they are being measured against. For your bonds, the benchmarks should have similar *average maturity* and *credit quality* characteristics.

Capable advisors have the tools to assess the overall risk of your portfolio given your particular choice of asset classes and weightings for each. By comparing your results to those of a comparable portfolio of indices or appropriate benchmarks (using the same weights for each comparable component), you will have the basis for making an informed assessment of your performance.

Again, keep in mind that **it is the performance of your portfolio as a whole that matters**.

CHAPTER 7

What about Alternatives?

We often hear about exclusive hedge funds, private equity funds, commodities, and other non-traditional investments. How are these investments different from the traditional asset classes we have recommended in this book? Should you include alternatives in your portfolio?

Diversity is Not Diversification

A common argument for including alternatives in a long-term portfolio is that they are good diversifiers, i.e., that they have good returns and a low correlation (they don't move in tandem) with traditional assets. While it is true that many alternatives are not highly correlated with standard investments, this fact alone is not sufficient to justify adding them to your portfolio. For example, the outcome of a bet on the Super Bowl has no correlation with stock market returns, but that doesn't mean betting on sports should be part of your investment portfolio!

There is little evidence that alternatives have higher returns than traditional asset classes. Our view is that many investors participating in alternative strategies (and even the managers of these strategies themselves) don't fully understand the risks they are taking.

Alternatives generally involve one or more of the following elements of increased risk:

- Using large amounts of borrowed money;
- Making concentrated bets;
- Trading excessively;
- Relying on subjective forecasts.

Exclusive is not Necessarily Excellent

Certain alternatives like hedge funds and private equity funds have very high minimum investment amounts that put their funds out of the reach of nearly all individual investors. This exclusivity can create an aura of mystery and attraction (it's just human nature). Some brokerage firms have taken advantage of this by putting together programs called *fund-of-funds* that allow smaller investors to pool their money together to gain access to otherwise unavailable strategies. Of course, the brokerage firms layer on additional fees for this privilege. The evidence shows that, on average, fund-of-funds underperform the primary funds in which they invest.[1]

We want to remind you that just because something is hard to get does not mean it is a good investment or appropriate for you. **You should think carefully before investing in a fund-of-funds strategy.**

Here are some commonly mentioned alternative investments:

HEDGE FUNDS

Hedge funds come in a variety of flavors and follow an extremely broad range of investment and trading strategies. For example, they make bets on global-macro trends, distressed debt, currency movements, commodities, corporate mergers, and they engage in short selling

---

[1] See Kat and Amin (2001), Amin and Kat (2002), Ackermann, McEnally and Ravenscraft (1999), Lhabitant and Learned (2002), Brown, Goetzmann and Liang (2004), Capocci and Hubner (2004), and Fung and Hsieh (2004).

(betting on price declines), among other strategies. Each of these strategies has a unique risk and return relationship. That's why, in the aggregate, we cannot consider hedge funds to be an asset class.

The three most common characteristics of hedge funds are that:

1. *Manager compensation* is high, typically 1.5 percent of assets and 20 percent of the profits above a certain hurdle rate;[2] and,

2. *Leverage* is often employed (borrowing against invested assets) to magnify returns;

3. *Liquidity* is low (there are usually restrictions on getting your money out).

As a result, we often read about managers earning billions for themselves and extraordinarily good returns for their investors. However, their excessive risk and high fees can also lead to extraordinarily bad results, as we regularly hear about the implosion of high profile hedge funds, especially in recent years.

The competitive landscape of hedge funds is rapidly changing, as hundreds of funds are opened and closed every year. For example, *Pensions & Investments* reported that 784 new funds were started in 2009, while 1,023 existing funds were closed. Amazingly, the median life of a hedge fund is only 31 months. Fewer than 15 percent of hedge funds last longer than six years, and 60 percent of them disappear in less than three years.[3]

Understanding the historical returns of hedge funds is difficult because the return databases have many problems. Managers provide their return information only when they want to (presumably when their returns are good), and funds with poor results that are closed are removed from the database entirely. Attempts to adjust for these deficiencies have shown that hedge fund returns are far lower than reported.

---

[2] Median fee structure, according to TASS Data.
[3] King, M.R., and Maier, P., 2009, "Hedge funds and financial stability: Regulating Prime Brokers will Mitigate Systemic Risks," *Journal of Financial Stability*, 5 p.285

The lack of persistency in the performance of hedge funds is similar to that of traditional active managers. The chance that a hedge fund that performed above average in one year will repeat in the following year is about 50%.[4] This is what you would expect by random chance.

Understand that **hedge funds are often (1) higher in cost, (2) less diversified, (3) more leveraged, and (4) less liquid** than traditional investments like mutual funds.

PRIVATE EQUITY (INCLUDING VENTURE CAPITAL)

Private equity funds take relatively small equity investments and large amounts of debt and invest in companies that are either already private (not publicly traded on the stock exchange) or will be taken private (through the buyout of a publicly traded company). The two most common private equity strategies are leveraged buyouts and venture capital.

Successful private equity firms add value by becoming directly involved in the management of the companies in which they invest to help drive greater efficiencies and growth. The objective is to sell a portfolio company for a large multiple of its initial investment, usually through an initial public offering, acquisition by another company, or recapitalization (when the company has generated enough value to borrow more and repay its owners).

It can take up to five or six years for a private equity firm to invest your money and years more to realize successful outcomes. Therefore, restrictions usually accompany an investor's ability to get his money out in the short term. Up to two percent management fees and twenty percent of the upside are common compensation arrangements for private equity managers.

Venture capital has comparable manager compensation arrangements and investor liquidity constraints. However, because venture capital

---

[4] Malkiel, B. G., and A. Saha 2005, "Hedge Funds: Risk and Return," *Financial Analysts Journal,* 61(6), pp.84-85.

investments are often made in start-up or early development companies that are riskier and may not have existing assets, the use of debt to magnify returns is not common.

Similar to hedge funds, it is difficult to assess the performance of the private equity industry as a whole because performance is reported on a voluntary basis. Academics have also identified two other concerns with private equity industry reported returns that cause those returns to be inflated: excessive valuation of ongoing investments and a bias toward better-performing funds.[5]

Understand that **private equity is generally (1) higher in cost, (2) less diversified, (3) more leveraged, and (4) less liquid** than traditional investments like mutual funds.

COMMODITIES (GOLD, OIL & GAS, ETC.)

Commodities include natural resources such as agricultural products (grains, food, and fiber), livestock and meat, precious and industrial metals (gold, silver, etc.), and energy (oil and gas). You can invest in commodities in a variety of ways such as through mutual funds, futures contracts (bets on the future price of a commodity), exchange traded funds, or direct ownership (usually impractical due to storage).

Commodity advocates will tell you that commodities serve as an inflation hedge and provide a diversification benefit. In short periods this can be true, but over the long term you should consider the following:

1. A good hedging vehicle is something that is *highly correlated* (moves together) with the risk you are trying to reduce, both in the short run and the long run. A well-diversified basket of commodities should be highly correlated with inflation over the very long run (in fact, this is basically how inflation is measured).

---

[5] Phalippou, Ludovic and Oliver Gottschalg, 2009, "Performance of Private Equity Funds," *The Review of Financial Studies,* Vol. 22, Issue 4, pp. 1747-1776.

In the short run, however, commodity prices can be very volatile — many times greater than that of inflation, which is very slow to change. Therefore **you run the risk of experiencing a big short-term gain or loss using commodities as an inflation hedge**. This may offset any potential hedging benefit.

2. Unlike traditional assets, commodities do not generate earnings, pay interest, or create business value. They are a speculative bet in which there is a winner and loser at the end of the trade. **No share of any earnings stream is to be had with commodities.** Moreover, a broad-based stock portfolio already has significant commodity exposure through ownership of companies involved in energy, mining, agriculture, natural resources, and refined products.

SUMMARY

Our belief is that **you don't need alternative investments in your portfolio to have a successful investment experience**, particularly considering their higher costs, lack of diversification, and liquidity constraints.

CHAPTER 8

Everyone
Can
Succeed

No doubt what you have just read contradicts nearly everything you have ever been told about investing. When most people think about investment advice, they think in terms of forecasting. Can you find someone with a crystal ball?

As you now understand, you do not have to predict the future to have a successful investment experience. This is because **with capitalism there is a positive return on capital**. Otherwise, it wouldn't be capitalism!

Investing is not about winning and losing. It is not a competitive sport. It is not the case that if we are right, we win and if we are wrong, we lose. There are not winners and losers in our capital markets, with the winners taking all the spoils and the losers going broke. Of course, in a capitalistic system some will get extremely rich and others will lose everything, but **everyone who takes the time to address these five investment decisions can have a successful investment experience**.

The elegant truth of economics is that the return on capital is exactly equal to the cost of capital. Wealth is created when natural resources, labor, intellectual capital, and financial capital combine to produce economic growth. As an investor, you are entitled to a share of that economic growth when your financial assets are invested in and used by the global economy.

This is not a free lunch. It is your fair share of profits as compensation for putting your money to work.

So how can you best capture your share? Again, we believe the most effective way is to deploy your capital throughout the public fixed income and equity markets in a broadly diversified manner designed to capture a global capital market rate of return. With the proper time horizon and discipline you can reach your financial goals and outperform most investors with less risk.

Remember, do not focus on what you cannot control. You cannot predict the occurrence of an event like the mortgage crisis, the sovereign debt crisis, or an oil spill in the Gulf of Mexico. However, together with your advisor you can control your costs, diversify properly, establish the right asset allocation, and maintain the discipline to stay the course. By following the recommendations in this book, you will have done everything possible to stack the investment odds in your favor.

Going forward, when you see the investment predictions on the cover of the latest financial periodical, watch the talking heads make their forecasts on TV, and listen to your friends and neighbors boast about their latest great investment scheme, you will understand that they are speculating instead of investing. Now you know a better way. **You have the answer.**

A Personal Note from the Authors

"Dan, I just got my scan results and they found another tumor. They said I have six months." That's what Gordon told me over the phone on June 8, 2010, while I was sitting in my hotel suite overlooking the Pacific Ocean in Monterrey, California, preparing to speak at an investment conference that night. For some reason, upon hearing this news I said to him, "Let's write that book you've always wanted to do."

He said that he didn't have it in him, but I told him that together we could do it. I was determined to get the book finished, printed, and in his hands. I was going to do this for my dear friend who had given me so much over the years.

I first met Gordon Murray in 2002, when he approached me to help him manage his family's investments. He was an experienced investor himself, having just retired from a 25-year career on Wall Street, where he interfaced with some of the largest and most sophisticated institutional investors in the world. We immediately became good friends and, over time, connected on a deeply personal level. We developed a special bond of trust and camaraderie that occurs rarely in life.

Gordon became enthralled with the idea that a global capital market rate of return is available to anyone–without subjective forecasting, stock picking or market timing–using broadly diversified investment vehicles in balanced portfolios: the antithesis of the traditional Wall Street approach. Having once considered himself a student of the markets when it came to investing, he was surprised to learn that his knowledge of capital markets was incomplete.

As long as I've known Gordon, he has had a passion for investing and for giving back to others. He's also had a growing frustration, as have I, with the way the existing financial services industry operates and how it treats investors. For years, he has been forwarding articles to me about investors who have been taken advantage of, or those who simply made poor decisions with their money and suffered terrible financial consequences as a result.

We both wanted to do something about this, and Gordon told me many times that he wanted to write a clear and concise book about our shared investment philosophy to help educate individual investors about the important aspects of personal investing—so that they can protect themselves and make smart financial decisions. That dream became a reality when we finished *The Investment Answer*.

The journey we've had together in writing this book has been extraordinary. We worked together beautifully, and I drew meaning from the fact that we were creating something that would not only become part of Gordon's legacy but also would help as many people as possible become more successful investors.

Dan Goldie
December 2010

I have been extremely lucky to have outlived my brain tumor survival expectations; luckier still to have had the time to plan and to experience closure and so much love from family and friends; and perhaps even luckier to have had the opportunity to give something back.

For decades, we have watched much of the traditional financial services industry (which includes money managers, the mainstream financial media, as well as Wall Street brokers) take advantage of innocent, hard-working investors' lack of financial expertise and their behavioral tendencies.

Deep down inside I knew there was a better way to invest. I knew about passive investing, of course. I knew about low-cost investing. But I did not realize that an individual investor could get these kinds of returns, not in theory but in practice, in an actual investment porfolio. This was amazing. When Dan laid it all out for me in his office in 2002, I thought, *This is it.*

Dan and I wrote this book to help everyday investors, and to fill a void that exists in today's investment literature. Our challenge was to distill, sequence, and articulate the best concepts of investing (not speculating) into an easy-to-read, concise, yet complete work. This book gives individual investors the essential knowledge base to help stack the investment odds in their favor.

The story behind *The Investment Answer* is one of friendship, love, dedication, and perseverance. The process of writing with Dan has been the most collaborative experience of my life. Because we knew each other's strengths, weaknesses, and personalities so well, there were no distractions or disagreements. Dan has really lifted me up and helped give special meaning to this last part of my life.

Gordon S. Murray
December 2010

About the Authors

Daniel C. Goldie

Mr. Goldie is President of Dan Goldie Financial Services LLC, a registered investment advisory firm that helps individual investors and families manage their money and make smart financial decisions. He has been recognized by the *San Francisco Business Times* as one of the top 25 Bay Area independent advisors, and by *Barron's* as one of the top 100 independent financial advisors in the United States.

In 1998, Mr. Goldie co-authored *The Prudent Investor's Guide to Beating Wall Street at Its Own Game*. He began his investment career in 1991 after retiring from the ATP Tour (men's professional tennis), where he was a Wimbledon quarterfinalist and won four professional titles. Mr. Goldie was the 1986 NCAA men's singles champion for Stanford University. He has been inducted into the Collegiate Tennis Hall of Fame, the Northern California Tennis Hall of Fame, and the Stanford University Sports Hall of Fame.

Mr. Goldie holds an A.B. in economics from Stanford University and an M.B.A. from The Walter A. Haas School of Business, University of California at Berkeley. He is a member of the CFA Institute and the CFA Society of San Francisco, and has earned the Chartered Financial Analyst designation and CERTIFIED FINANCIAL PLANNER™ certification.

Gordon S. Murray

Mr. Murray spent over 25 years working on Wall Street, primarily at Goldman Sachs, Lehman Brothers, and Credit Suisse First Boston, in a variety of institutional sales and management roles. In sales, he covered some of the largest and most sophisticated institutional investors in the world. As a manager, he worked across all product areas and saw firsthand how these once proud institutions lost their way through the excessive use of leverage, overly complex products, proprietary trading, and by not putting their clients first.

After his Wall Street career, Mr. Murray worked as a consultant with Dimensional Fund Advisors, an investment management firm known for bringing academic research to the practical world of investing. In that role, he helped independent, fee-only advisors articulate the merits of investing versus speculating.

Mr. Murray has served on the board of the Hillsborough Schools Foundation where he founded the Scholars' Circle. Currently he is a Vice-Chair of the U.C. Berkeley Parents' Fund and Advisory Board where he received the Trustees Citation Award in 2009. Mr. Murray graduated from the University of North Carolina at Chapel Hill with an A.B. in Political Science, and received an M.B.A. from Columbia University.

Appendix

Hypothetical Portfolio Weights

	FIXED	DEFENSIVE	CONSERVATIVE	MODERATE	AGGRESSIVE	EQUITY
EQUITY	0%	20%	40%	60%	80%	100%
US STOCKS	0%	14%	28%	42%	56%	70%
LARGE CAP S&P 500 INDEX	0.0	4.0	8.0	12.0	16.0	20.0
LARGE CAP VALUE FAMA /FRENCH US LARGE CAP VALUE INDEX	0.0	4.0	8.0	12.0	16.0	20.0
SMALL CAP FAMA /FRENCH US SMALL CAP INDEX	0.0	2.0	4.0	6.0	8.0	10.0
SMALL CAP VALUE FAMA /FRENCH US SMALL CAP VALUE INDEX	0.0	2.0	4.0	6.0	8.0	10.0
REAL ESTATE STRATEGY DOW JONES US SELECT REIT INDEX	0.0	2.0	4.0	6.0	8.0	10.0
NON-US STOCKS	0%	6%	12%	18%	24%	30%
VALUE FAMA /FRENCH INTERNATIONAL VALUE INDEX	0.0	2.0	4.0	6.0	8.0	10.0
SMALL CAP INTERNATIONAL SMALL CAP INDEX	0.0	1.0	2.0	3.0	4.0	5.0
SMALL CAP VALUE INTERNATIONAL SMALL CAP VALUE INDEX	0.0	1.0	2.0	3.0	4.0	5.0
EMERGING MARKETS MSCI EMERGING MARKETS INDEX	0.0	0.6	1.2	1.8	2.4	3.0
EMERGING MARKETS VALUE FAMA/FRENCH EMERGING MARKETS VALUE INDEX	0.0	0.6	1.2	1.8	2.4	3.0
EMERGING MARKETS SMALL CAP FAMA /FRENCH EMERGING MARKETS SMALL CAP INDEX	0.0	0.8	1.6	2.4	3.2	4.0
FIXED INCOME	100%	80%	60%	40%	20%	0%
ONE -YEAR MERRILL LYNCH ONE -YEAR US TREASURY NOTE INDEX	25.0	20.0	15.0	10.0	5.0	0.0
TWO-YEAR GLOBAL CITIGROUP WORLD GOVERNMENT BOND INDEX 1-3 YEARS (HEDGED)	25.0	20.0	15.0	10.0	5.0	0.0
FIVE-YEAR GOVERNMENT BARCLAYS CAPITAL TREASURY BOND INDEX 1-5 YEARS	25.0	20.0	15.0	10.0	5.0	0.0
FIVE-YEAR GLOBAL CITIGROUP WORLD GOVERNMENT BOND INDEX 1-5 YEARS (HEDGED)	25.0	20.0	15.0	10.0	5.0	0.0

For illustrative purposes only. Past performance is no guarantee of future results. These hypothetical portfolios are not recommendations for an actual allocation. Indices are not available for direct investment and their performance does not reflect the expenses of an actual portfolio. Real Estate Stocks weighting allocated evenly between US Small Cap and US Small Cap Value prior to January 1978 data inception. International Value weighting allocated evenly between International Small Cap and MSCI EAFE Index (net dividends) prior to January 1975 data inception. International Small Cap Value weighting allocated to International Small Cap prior to July 1981 data inception. Emerging Markets weighting allocated evenly between International Small Cap and International Value prior to January 1988 data inception. Emerging Markets Value and Small Cap weighting allocated evenly between International Small Cap and International Value prior to January 1989 data inception. Two-Year Global weighting allocated to One-Year prior to January 1990 data inception. Five-Year Government weighting allocated to Barclays Capital US Government Bond Index Intermediate prior to January 1976 data inception. Five-Year Global weighting allocated to Five-Year Government prior to January 1990 data inception.

SOURCES AND DESCRIPTIONS OF DATA

US Equities

Fama/French US Small Cap Index

Fama/French US Small Cap Index provided by Fama/French from CRSP securities data. Includes the lower-half range in market cap of NYSE securities (plus NYSE Amex equivalents since July 1962 and Nasdaq equivalents since 1973).

S&P 500 Index

Provided by Standard & Poor's Index Services Group. "Standard & Poor's®," "S&P®," "S&P 500®," Standard & Poor's 500®," and "500" are trademarks of the McGraw-Hill Companies, Inc.

Fama/French US Small Cap Value Index

Fama/French US Small Value Index provided by Fama/French from CRSP securities data. Includes the lower-half range in market cap and the upper 30% in book-to-market of NYSE securities (plus NYSE Amex equivalents since July 1962 and Nasdaq equivalents since 1973), excluding utilities.

Fama/French US Large Cap Value Index

Fama/French US Large Value Index provided by Fama/French from CRSP securities data Includes the upper-half range in market cap and the upper 30% in book-to-market of NYSE securities (plus NYSE Amex equivalents since July 1962 and Nasdaq equivalents since 1973), excluding utilities.

Fama/French US Small Cap Growth Index

Fama/French US Small Growth Index provided by Fama/French from CRSP securities data. Includes the lower-half range in market cap and the lower 30% in book-to-market of NYSE securities (plus NYSE Amex equivalents since July 1962 and Nasdaq equivalents since 1973), excluding utilities.

Fama/French US Large Cap Growth Index

Fama/French US Large Growth Index provided by Fama/French from CRSP securities data. Includes the upper-half range in market cap and the lower 30% in book-to-market of NYSE securities (plus NYSE Amex equivalents since July 1962 and Nasdaq equivalents since 1973), excluding utilities.

CRSP Deciles 1-5 Index

Center for Research in Securities Prices, University of Chicago. Large company universe returns (deciles 1-5). October 1988-present: CRSP Deciles 1-5 cap-based portfolio. January 1973-September 1988: CRSP database (NYSE & AMEX & OTC), rebalanced quarterly. July 1962-December 1972: CRSP database (NYSE & AMEX), rebalanced quarterly. January 1926-June 1962: NYSE, rebalanced semi-annually.

CRSP Deciles 6-10 Index

Center for Research in Securities Prices, University of Chicago. Small company universe returns (deciles 6-10). October 1988-present: CRSP Deciles 6-10 cap-based portfolio. January 1973-September 1988: CRSP database (NYSE & AMEX & OTC), rebalanced quarterly. July 1962-December 1972: CRSP database (NYSE & AMEX), rebalanced quarterly. January 1926-June 1962: NYSE, rebalanced semi-annually.

Dow Jones US Select REIT Index

Provided by Dow Jones Indexes.

International Equities

International Small Cap Index

1994-present: Dimensional International Small Cap Index compiled by Dimensional from Bloomberg securities data. Includes securities of MSCI World ex-US countries in the bottom 10% range of market capitalization; market-capitalization weighted; each company is capped at 5%; rebalanced annually. July 1981-1993: Compiled by Dimensional from StyleResearch securities data. Includes securities in the bottom 10% range of market capitalization, excluding the bottom 1%; market-capitalization weighted; each country is capped at 50%; rebalanced semiannually. 1970-June 1981: 50% UK Small Cap Index and 50% Japan Small Cap Index (see below).

MSCI EAFE Index

MSCI EAFE Index (net dividends) © MSCI 2010, all rights reserved.

Japan Small Cap Index

1994-present: Dimensional Japan Small Cap Index compiled by Dimensional from Bloomberg securities data. Includes Japanese securities in the bottom 10%

range of market capitalization; market capitalization weighted; each company is capped at 10%; excludes REITs; rebalanced annually. July 1981-1993: Compiled by Dimensional from StyleResearch securities data. Includes Japanese securities in the bottom 10% range of market capitalization, excluding the bottom 1%; market capitalization weighted; rebalanced semiannually. 1970-June 1981: Nomura Japanese Small Companies Index provided by Nomura Securities Investment Trust Management Company, Ltd., Tokyo. Includes securities of Tokyo Stock Exchange in the smaller half of the first section; market-capitalization weighted; rebalanced semiannually.

United Kingdom Small Cap Index

1994-present: Dimensional UK Small Cap Index compiled from Bloomberg securities data. Includes UK securities in the bottom 10% range of market capitalization; market-capitalization weighted; each company is capped at 10%; excludes REITs; rebalanced annually. July 1981-1993: Compiled by Dimensional from StyleResearch securities data. Includes UK securities in the bottom 10% range of market capitalization, excluding the bottom 1%; market-capitalization weighted; rebalanced semiannually. 1956-June 1981: Hoare Govett Smaller Companies Index provided by the London Business School and ABN AMRO. Includes securities of London Stock Exchange in the bottom 10% of market capitalization of fully listed UK stocks; market-capitalization weighted; rebalanced annually.

Fama-French International Value Index

2008-present: Fama/French International Value Index provided by Fama/ French from Bloomberg securities data. Simulated strategy of MSCI EAFE countries in the upper 30% book-to-market range. 1975-2007: Provided by Fama/French from MSCI securities data.

International Small Cap Value Index

1994-present: Dimensional International Small Cap Value Index compiled by Dimensional from StyleResearch securities data. Includes securities of MSCI World ex US countries in the bottom 10% range of market capitalization and in the upper 30% book-to-market range; market-capitalization weighted; each company is capped at 5%; excludes REITs and utilities; rebalanced annually. 1982-1993: Compiled by Dimensional from StyleResearch securities data. Includes securities in the bottom 10% range of market capitalization, excluding the bottom 1%, and in the upper 30% book-to-market range; market-capitalization weighted; each country is capped at 50%; rebalanced semiannually.

MSCI Emerging Markets Index

MSCI Emerging Markets Index (gross dividends) © MSCI 2010, all rights reserved.

Fama/French Emerging Markets Value Index

2009: Provided by Fama/French from Bloomberg securities data. Simulated strategy using IFC investable universe countries. Companies in the upper 30% of aggregate market cap; companies weighted by float-adjusted market cap; countries weighted by country float-adjusted market cap; rebalanced monthly. 1989-2008: Provided by Fama/French from IFC securities data. IFC data provided by International Finance Corporation.

Fama/French Emerging Markets Small Cap Index

Provided by Fama/French from Bloomberg securities data. Simulated strategy using IFC investable universe countries. Companies in the bottom 30% of aggregate market cap; companies weighted by float-adjusted market cap; countries weighted by country float-adjusted market cap; rebalanced monthly. 1989-2008: Provided by Fama/French from IFC securities data. IFC data provided by International Finance Corporation.

Fixed Income

Long-Term Government Bonds

©Stocks, Bonds, Bills, and Inflation Yearbook™, Ibbotson Associates, Chicago (annually updated work by Roger G. Ibbotson and Rex A. Sinquefield). Includes US government bonds with an average maturity of twenty years.

Barclays Capital US Government/Credit Bond Index Intermediate

Provided by Barclays Bank PLC.

One-Month US Treasury Bills

©Stocks, Bonds, Bills, and Inflation Yearbook™, Ibbotson Associates, Chicago (annually updated work by Roger G. Ibbotson and Rex A. Sinquefield).

Merrill Lynch One-Year US Treasury Note Index

Used with permission; copyright 2010 Merrill Lynch, Pierce, Fenner & Smith Incorporated; all rights reserved. The Merrill Lynch Indices may not be copied, used, or distributed without Merrill Lynch's prior written approval.

Citigroup World Government Bond Index 1-3 Years (hedged)

Copyright 2010 by Citigroup.

Citigroup World Government Bond Index 1-5 Years (hedged)

Copyright 2010 by Citigroup.

Barclays Capital Treasury Bond Index 1-5 Years

Provided by Barclays Bank PLC.

Barclays Capital US Government Bond Index Intermediate

Provided by Barclays Bank PLC.

Inflation

Inflation: Changes in the Consumer Price Index

©Stocks, Bonds, Bills, and Inflation Yearbook™, Ibbotson Associates, Chicago (annually updated work by Roger G. Ibbotson and Rex A. Sinquefield). Used with permission. All rights reserved.

Index